IVORY BOOKS
UK | UAE | INDIA

Published by
Ivory Books Ltd.
9 Edinburg Drive, Ickenham
Uxbridge, England, UB108QY

ISBN : 978-1-7391433-0-5

Printed and bound in India by
Anaswara Offset Printers,
Kochi, Kerala, India

www.ivorybooks.uk

BUSINESS GITA

AJAYYA KUMAR

Research & Illustration:
Elizabeth Shilpa Abraham

IVORY BOOKS
UXBRIDGE, ENGLAND

Contents

Introduction

I have often wondered and debated with myself what could be the best form of communication. From papyrus scrolls and bottled messages, the human race has certainly come a long way. Those days when I eagerly waited for letters from grandparents and poured out my heart to the pen pal whom I've never met are long gone. Today my daughter texts from her room upstairs that she would take another five minutes to be at the dinner table. I get real-time updates on what's happening around the world. The smell, touch and feel of my hardbound books have been more or less replaced by the icy coldness of kindles and iPads. The dramatic way in which the communication scenario and information consumption habits of people changed over the last few years have often left me confused about what would be the most effective way in which I can communicate my thoughts to the world.

I found the answer almost a year back in my favourite book of all times - Bhagavad Gita. Written many centuries ago, Gita still shows way to millions during their most critical junctures and offers them solace, comfort, confidence and enlightenment. It comprises 700 verses which are conversations between Lord Krishna and Arjuna, some of which have been a guiding light to me all along my life. I have by now lost count of how many times I have read and re-read these conversations and it was during one such occasion that it struck me; isn't the most effective form of communication, after all, a conversation? They are short, informal, less intimidating and have a personal touch. Their intimate nature gives the reader a certain sense of closeness. What more to say about the effectiveness of conversations when a chat over a coffee marks the beginning of some lifelong relationships!

Thus, like how Krishna showed Arjuna the reality of things, Gita also helped me clear my confusions too. In my moment of truth, I knew conversations would be my medium to talk to the larger world around me and impart my knowledge and experience to others. These are a select bunch of conversations I have had with my family, friends, colleagues, acquaintances and myself at different points in my life. I'm an entrepreneur, but what I have to tell the world is not just limited to entrepreneurship or business. It's an assorted mix of everything I would like to talk about, know about and in my opinion, every entrepreneur should care about. I hope you like it.

Foreword

The Bhagavad Gita (Sanskrit: "Song of God") is an extraordinary 700-verse epic that emerged in written form some 2000 years ago in India. It is probably much older than that. Revered by Hindus, it is much more than their spiritual text. It is a moral and philosophical treatise and a code of conduct for all humanity, regardless of religion and culture. At its core, is the question: what constitutes the virtuous path for us?

Ajayya Kumar's remarkably engaging little book is for entrepreneurs. Not just in the business profit sense of the term but for all who seek to live and interact with others with mutual benefit. What are the qualities of leadership and relationship needed in today's world? What is the ethical way of doing business? What is success and how do we achieve it?

Although Ajayya draws inspiration from millennium old wisdom, his prescriptions are bang up-to-date for our age of the internet, social media, Covid and climate change. It deserves a place next to one's laptop where it can be easily consulted when, as often happens, doubt and confusion clouds one's judgement on how to do the right things in the right way.

Professor Mukesh Kapila, CBE

Jnana

Leadership

"Whatever action a great man performs, common men follow. And whatever standards he sets by exemplary acts, all the world pursues."

1. The leader who flaws

Ajay: What's happening at school these days, dear?

Jahnavi: A new teacher has joined, Papa. Yesterday, while she was teaching us, one of my classmates asked her a question to which she didn't know the answer. She said she will refer and get back to us. The whole class is now talking behind her back.

Ajay: But why?

Jahnavi: What kind of a teacher needs to look it up when she is asked a doubt?

Ajay: The kind of teacher who didn't let her ego get in the way of passing on the correct information to her students.

Jahnavi: But isn't a teacher supposed to know everything? What if your employees approach you for the right judgement and you don't have one? Isn't this like that?

Ajay: Neither your teacher nor your father is omnipotent dear. We are imperfect human beings. But what makes one a great leader is when s/he recognises his/her flaws and not let those flaws affect the larger scheme of things.

Jahnavi: How does someone's personal flaws affect the larger scheme of things?

Ajay: How many students are there in your class?

Jahnavi: 50

Ajay: When your classmate raised his doubt, what if the teacher got insecure and decided to mask it at any cost? All fifty of you would have ended up with wrong info, right? Or what if she was the controlling type and silenced the boy who raised the question? You will all be apprehensive to ask questions in the future and grow up into adults who would not question anything. Similarly, even in business, when a leader is insecure, controlling, impulsive or overconfident, it impacts the functioning of the whole organisation negatively.

Jahnavi: Why didn't I think this way before! My respect has doubled now, for my teacher as well as for my papa.

2. Are you micromanaging your team?

Rakhi (to daughter): Is that the dress you picked for tomorrow's function? Not very impressive. Come, I'll pick one for you.

Ajay: Our girls are growing up Rakhi. You should give them a little more autonomy and respect their choices.

Rakhi: But I'm their mom and I know what's best for them.

Ajay: You are a wonderful mother. But micromanaging is a controlling behaviour which is counter productive.

Rakhi: How so?

Ajay: Because you convert your children into individuals who are not capable of making decisions for themselves in the future. The same is applicable in organisations too. Among several business leaders and team managers I have seen the tendency to control every aspect of the employee's functioning.

Rakhi: Hmm ... I understand. From the employee's point of view that would mean a lack of faith in his work, which would affect his motivation to work itself.

Ajay: Exactly. To micromanage is to question his competence and deny his autonomy. This could render the employee aloof, affecting his productivity and leading to increased employee attrition at a larger level.

Rakhi: I'm happy that you pointed it out when I was beginning to micromanage.

Ajay: I'm not above flaws either. Micromanaging gives us the illusion of power which is what most humans seek. Besides, we all have multiple insecurities, emotional complexities and challenges in the family as well as at the workplace, from which this kind of behaviour stems.

Rakhi: I guess the key then is to be conscious always.

Ajay: Yes. Educating yourself about human nature and what kind of strategies work best would be helpful. It would also be good to get feedback from others on how you treat them or the areas in which you can improve. Be it family or workplace, you get the best results when you make everybody feel belonged and part of one wonderful team.

3. Leaders should think like a follower too

Ajay: That's a pretty big poster of the superstar on your desk. Are you a fan?

Rajith: Oh, I'm his biggest fan! But lately his movies have been bombing at the box office. Even a hardcore fan like me couldn't digest his latest one.

Ajay: That's sad.

Rajith: I just don't get it. Are we wrong to think that people like him, after all these years of acting and accolades, would be able to spot a bad script when they see one?

Ajay: Many factors could have played a role here - his previous commitments, relations in the industry, a good script going bad in the hands of the director... But a big reason could be that he has stopped thinking like a follower.

Rajith: What do you mean?

Ajay: There's this widespread notion that there are two kinds of people - those who think like leaders and those who think like followers. But I don't entirely agree with it. We are living in a world of fluid identities and it's important that a leader also thinks like a follower to get a sense of the changing workspace sentiments and to understand the pulse of the larger mass.

Rajith: I guess it's not easy.

Ajay: Well, one has to try to not let the stardom or the power that comes with leadership not get into your head. Because, without that connect with your followers who constitute the larger world out there, you start growing comfortable in your own 'leadership' echo chamber unaware of the changing dynamics outside. In no time things will come crumbling down.

Rajith: That's a valuable lesson not just for the superstar, but even for people like me, Ajay.

Ajay: You are the budding stars of tomorrow. As you grow, make forceful efforts to think like a follower. Evaluate your actions by taking a step back. Embrace the duality of being a leader and follower at the same time.

4. Why sensitive leadership matters

Ajay:	Hey! Sorry that I'm late.
Ajit:	No problem. I got your text. All okay at the office?
Ajay:	One of my colleagues has been going through some issues in personal life and had a meltdown today at the office. So some of us stayed back to help him through it.
Ajit:	Oh what a weakling! Just ask him to pull it together and power through.
Ajay:	I don't think it's that easy. When you fall ill, do you seek help or ask yourself to power through it?
Ajit:	But this is different.
Ajay:	What makes you think mental health is less important than physical health?
Ajit:	It's important. But as a leader don't you think you need to portray yourself as tough and strong?

Ajay: Well, I would like to think of myself as more of a sensitive and compassionate leader. Strength is not about turning your back to others' problems, which is actually quite easy to do. What takes guts is to be compassionate, to show your vulnerable side.

Ajit: How can a leader be seen as vulnerable? If the commandant is seen as vulnerable, it demotivates the spirit of the soldiers.

Ajay: The world is changing and we need to stop equating this to some kind of war. 'Dukkha' or suffering is one of three markers of human life according to Buddhism. Then why should we ignore it and harp on toxic positivity? It rains and shines in all of our lives. So, it's unrealistic to expect someone to always be motivated and stay energised.

Ajit: Hmm.. I think that makes sense.

Ajay: Society puts so much pressure on us to always appear positive and I think it's doing more damage than good leading to emotional repression. Unfortunately it has been the work culture at several companies. But we are living in a world which is growing more sensitive day by day.

Ajit: So you are saying your sensitive approach has been working?

Ajay: Definitely! It has helped build loyalty and boosted productivity among our employees. It brings out the human in us, makes our bonds stronger and helps us move together towards our common goal.

5. Short term wins vs Long term vision

Ajay: Long time, old friend. How are you?

Friend : I'm fine, Ajay. I have been striving to make this mission of mine a reality.

Ajay: Yes, I heard about it; Your dream to build a world class educational institution. So proud of you. How is it going?

Friend: It's going okay. But to be frank there are challenges too. We are yet to get some of the required licences and approvals; I need not tell you why.

Ajay: That is a tough challenge.

Friend: I'm sure we'll secure those soon. But there's something else that I need to address right away.

Ajay: What's that?

Friend: Attrition. Since it has been a while and many of the approvals are not yet in place, people are starting to feel demotivated. That's now causing an increase in flux. They don't see the larger vision I believe in.

Ajay: Hmm … I think as much as a larger vision is important, it's also crucial that you show them short term wins. People need to see results for the work they are doing and studies show that they start to get demotivated within 12-24 months if they don't see it. So, maybe that's something you need to work on while you keep trying for the approvals.

Friend: I may have forgotten about the importance of short term wins while pursuing the long term vision.

Ajay: There are so many things premium educational institutions do other than just teaching - advocacy, consultancy for government projects, collaborative works … you are the expert, you know it better.

Friend: You are right.

Ajay: So, set yearly goals related to these and reward and acknowledge people who achieve the objectives. Everybody may not be as passionate or patient as you towards the long term vision, so these kinds of short term goals are very critical to maintain the same level of commitment and interest of the staff. Give it a try.

6. The power of communicating your vision

Friend: Ajay, I'm leaving a little early today.
Ajay: All okay?

Friend: Not in the best of my spirits. Frequent fights with my teenager.
Ajay: Want to talk?

Friend: What to say… I was raised as an entitled male. But I'm no longer one. And I'm trying to be different from my parents so that my son would be a responsible, conscious, and sensitive adult someday, fit for a world that's progressing fast. But he just resists all my efforts. The more I try to tell him, the more he becomes irresponsible at home.
Ajay: He thinks you are trying to control him over unnecessary silly things?

Friend: Exactly.
Ajay: Welcome to parenthood! But also, how effective do you think your communication to him has been?

Friend: As in?

Ajay: For example, the way he sees it, you criticise him for not picking up his socks or leaving his plates unwashed. But does he understand that the issue here is not a smelly sock or a dirty plate? Have you conveyed to him that your end goal is to make him part of a progressive value system and to ensure that he isn't left out in the future?

Friend: Ummm...

Ajay: Try doing that. We are living in the age of business transformations, aren't we? Some of them succeed, some of them fail. If you examine the successful ones, you can see how effectively they communicated the vision and the larger goal to the employees. Without your staff you can't succeed. And what motivates them is the knowledge that their efforts would bring about a larger, long term and useful change.

Friend: I get it now. It never occurred to me to do the same in my family.

Ajay: There's still time. Under-communicating could cause immense damage in family as well as business. So make sure you not only make your life your message, but also effectively pass on that message to those around you.

Secrets to success

"We are kept from our goal not by obstacles but by a clear path to a lesser goal."

1. Change is the only constant

Ajay: Hi Modrek! Great to see you!

Modrek: Hey Ajay! How are you? Long time no see!

Ajay: You're wearing gloves! Why?

Modrek: Call me paranoid but I want to remain safe. When I meet people, they want to shake hands, and I don't want to. But that would be so rude!

Ajay: Maybe there's a better answer to your problem than wearing gloves. Have you thought of that?

Modrek: I don't know... I wish there was a way out.

Ajay: Even world leaders are avoiding shaking hands. They join hands, bow, wave or even do fist bumps.

Modrek: Wow! That's a game changer. If they do it, then others will do it too.

Ajay: After all, the only constant changes. If we change our clothes according to the weather and situation, then why not manners and gestures?

Modrek: You are right, but greetings like shaking hands come so naturally. It's second nature.

Ajay: How about I tell you a story and then you can decide for yourself — hand in glove (pun intended) or not?

Modrek: Yes, that's a wonderful idea! And I might even find a solution to my problem.

Ajay: Once two brothers lived in a very cold place. They hunted in the summer to survive the winters. This was what they had learnt from their parents. But over the past few years, the weather was becoming colder and there wasn't enough game. So, the elder brother said they should move to a warmer area. But the second brother said they had always lived in that area as their parents had taught them. He didn't want to move away. In the end, the elder brother moved away. The younger one stayed put but his food ran out. By that time, all the mountain passes were blocked and he couldn't get help. He sadly perished. All of us have to adapt to changing realities. It's the only way forward.

Modrek: That's true! Even world leaders have changed, why can't I?

Ajay: Of course, if you want to continue wearing gloves, that's your choice.

Modrek: Oh no! So the next time someone wants to shake hands, I'll use my fist, in a good way!

2. Back to school lessons

Earlier this week, during my regular video call with family members in Kerala, I noticed that my usually-chirpy niece seemed all sullen.

"Your niece here has gotten too comfortable with online classes and is sulking about having to go back to school starting November 1," said my sister laughing.

"Aaha, let me talk to her," I said. We had an interesting conversation which went on like this.

Niece:	Hello uncle, have an interesting story for me this time too?
Ajay:	Haha, no dear, no story this time. But I have a question for you.
Niece:	What's that?
Ajay:	What do you wish to become when you grow up?
Niece:	A successful entrepreneur
Ajay:	That's flattering! You know, I picked up many of my skills that helped me as an entrepreneur from my classrooms.

Niece: What does the classroom offer that online class doesn't?

Ajay: Tell me this, when was the last time you helped a friend do an assignment or sought help from a friend to complete your group project or had to overcome your fears to present a seminar in front of your entire class?

Niece: Umm.. I think when I was in school. But isn't it good that I can present a seminar sitting in my comfort zone instead of doing it in front of the whole class?

Ajay: Is it? Because to be an entrepreneur is to get out of your comfort zone. Physical classroom shapes your communication skills, interpersonal skills, leadership capabilities, ability to tackle challenges and social skills like no virtual classroom can. In front of the screen, you are just you. In the classroom you are a team player and a social being. I don't think I need to tell you how important all of those are to growing as an entrepreneur.

Niece: Yeah, I get it

Ajay: You need to be careful and cautious of course in the current situation. At the policy level too it should be ensured that all precautions are in place. If those can be assured, then it's high time you get back to school.

Niece: You are right. I guess I grew too comfortable and didn't realise how much I have been missing my school and friends. I can't wait to meet them now!

3. Lessons from the minister's lamp

Intern 1: I'm craving for a pizza!

Intern 2: Ooohh pizza! Let's call this place from where we ordered last time.

Intern 1: I already did, but they are accepting only cash now and I don't carry cash around with me these days.

Intern 2: Me neither. Oh wait, I have a few bucks remaining from the fund we collected for our college anniversary celebrations. Let's use that.

Ajay: Umm...sorry for overhearing. But do you think it's a good idea to use money earmarked for something else for your personal needs?

Intern 2: Well.. Sir ... We didn't happen to have the cash right now. I can replace it as soon as I reach home. Moreover, it's just two pizzas. Not a big sum anyway.

Ajay: Okay.. but if your cravings can wait for a few minutes, shall I interest you in a story?

Intern 1: Of course!

Ajay: Once a king appointed a new minister. He then assigned another person to keep an eye on the minister. One day the person approached the minister to test him and told him he wanted to discuss something beneficial to the minister. The minister asked the man to return in the evening as it was his working hours. So the man came back after it became dark to see the minister still engrossed in work. When he was done finally, the minister snuffed the oil lamp, took it inside and came back with another lamp. Curious to see this, the other person enquired why he changed the lamps.

Intern 1: I'm curious too.

Ajay: "I received the first lamp from the king for professional use. But now since we are about to discuss personal matters, I would only use my lamp," said the minister.

Intern 2: Wow! A man of integrity!

Ajay: Exactly my point. If you use a few bucks from the money reserved for something else, probably it's not going to make any difference. But, although small, you make a compromise on your integrity. Eventually such compromises will grow in size and ultimately would undermine your personal as well as professional growth.

Intern 2: I get your point.

Ajay: Great! Now who wants some pizza? This time it's on me!

4. Do you have plans A, B, C?

Ajay: Hi Dmitry! Why so tense?

Dmitry : Oh! Hi Ajay! It's just that my phone doesn't seem to be working and I was expecting a confirmation from a new customer.

Ajay: Let's see your phone. Hmm... the phone is fine. Only Facebook and WhatsApp are not working because their servers are down.

Dmitry : Oh no! I am in deep trouble. If my new customer confirms and I don't come to know about it, I will lose their business. I've just started my online business and this was my first large order.

Ajay: Social media is great! I myself am a big fan and use it throughout the day. But all the apps are network-based finally and disruptions can happen. Having a Plan B or a backup is a basic tenet of not only business but also life. The Covid pandemic has taught us all at least that much. Even the greatest kings and Gods have some weak points.

Dmitry: I did all my business on FB. It was working perfectly. I never thought that this could happen.

Ajay: In life, we create backups all the time because we know that things can go wrong. Nobody is invincible. There are thousands of examples of even the mighty falling. Alexander was defeated and so was Hitler. The Titanic sank. You can't drive a car out of a showroom without getting insurance; even the fittest man knows that his body will become weak one day; earthquakes reduce the height of mountains; a terror attack and high fuel prices drove America's largest international airline Pan Am to bankruptcy; Netflix and other streaming services could be the end of movie theatres; electric vehicles may soon fully replace fossil fuel-based vehicles...

Dimitry : I never thought that way. Let me see if I can find the client's details online and then contact them.

Ajay: And remember to create a Plan B or even a Plan C.

5. The man who pursued the elephant

Ajay: Hey! Good news! I heard the celebrity you had been pursuing to endorse your brand is in town next week for a show. This might be your best chance to meet him in person and ink a deal.

Priya: Thanks Ajay. But I gave up on that plan.

Ajay: But why! I think he is the best choice for your brand.

Priya: I think so too. But I exchanged a few emails with his team and they didn't seem very keen.

Ajay: C'mon! A few emails? Show some spirit! Be that man who wanted the elephant!

Priya: Huh? Who?

Ajay: Let me interest you with a story. There was a man who used to see an elephant and its mahout every morning on his way to work. Every day he would ask the mahout if he would give away the elephant. And every time the mahout would deny. Another man, who got curious seeing this, walked upto the first man and asked, "The mahout's reply is always going to be a 'no'. Then why do you still ask?" The first man smiled and said, "His answer has been 'no' till now. But what if tomorrow he says 'yes?'"

Priya: How optimistic!

Ajay: To be an entrepreneur is to be like him, my friend. Be relentless! So what if a couple of emails didn't work? Keep at it, meet him in person, make it work. Show him the dream you have, show him how you are building it. And if you don't get a 'yes,' you don't lose anything. But if you get a 'yes'...

Priya: I win an elephant! Wow! Never thought of it that way. Thanks Ajay, let me right away get a meeting fixed up with him.

6. See opportunity in everything

Ajay: Hey, how's the business going?

Murtuza : What to say Ajay, I had so many hopes and dreams when I started up early last year. But then the pandemic struck and now the business is struggling to stay afloat. I'm thinking of shutting it down and taking up a job. Would you have some role for me or refer me to someone?

Ajay: Of Course! But are you sure that's what you want to do? You might be in choppy waters now, but I'm sure great heights await you if you successfully tide over them. Trust me, no job can be as rewarding as being an entrepreneur.

Murtuza : I'm sure. But there's so much happening around us and managing a business amid all that sometimes seems overwhelming.

Ajay: Your answer is in what you said just now. There's so much happening around us. All you need to do is to tweak your business to make gains from whatever is happening around you.

Murtuza : How?

Ajay: I was reading this article which talks about how Black-owned bookstores saw sales shooting up after the 'Black Lives Matter' movement. Who knew a cause like that would benefit businesses! So you see, there's a business opportunity in even the seemingly unlikely ones. Small shops who went out of business during the lockdown started selling masks to stay afloat. Restaurants which would have otherwise shut shop started offering takeaways and got listed on food delivery platforms. Every crisis, every cause, every development is an opportunity for an entrepreneur, my friend. Your success would totally depend on how agile you are and how quickly you can spot the diamond in the rough. So, why don't you give it a try?

7. The rule of monthly surprises

Ajay: Hey! Are those dark circles beneath your eyes?

Rajeev: Oh that's nothing. My team threw a surprise party yesterday night for crossing the milestone of our first 1000 customers. It was almost early morning by the time the party was over.

Ajay: Haha! That's fun. So I guess you like surprises?

Rajeev: Who doesn't?

Ajay: In that case, what if every month you are not only surprised, but those surprises also help your business grow beyond your expectations?

Rajeev: That's insane! Who can give such surprises?

Ajay: You yourself.

Rajeev: What?? I don't understand.

Ajay: Call it the rule of monthly surprises if you like. As a budding entrepreneur this will help you grow, explore more avenues and enjoy what you are doing. Just surprise yourself every month.

Rajeev: Intriguing. How do I do that?

Ajay: Many ways. You usually have an idea about yourself, how you think, how you make decisions, how much you can work, what goals you can achieve in a month and so on, and you work accordingly, right? What if once in a month you do it a bit differently?

Make a decision that's unlike your usual ones. Try a different strategy. Take a risk that you have been unwilling to. Outdo your monthly targets. Send a 'hello' to that investor who you thought was too big for your startup. Walk to your office instead of driving. Take stairs instead of the lift. Smell a lily instead of your usual roses.

Rajeev: That sounds wonderful!

Ajay: Don't bother about surprising the customers or the board or your team. This is all about you. Give it a shot and you will find your confidence level going up. You will work harder, better and your productivity levels will be much higher.

Inclusion

"He who is deluded by the ego thinks, I am the doer."

1. Work from home - a boon or a curse?

Ajay: Hey, long time no see. Why are you not visiting the club these days? You used to be one of the most active members.

Natasha: Hey, Ajay! Earlier I used to drop by the club on the way back home from the office. But after Covid struck, I have been working from home entirely.

Ajay: Oh! How do you feel about the whole work from home thing?

Natasha: In a way it's quite convenient. But the flip side is that it has cut me off from my social circles and limited my human interactions.

Ajay: I understand. I agree there should be more flexibility for those who need it, but when it comes to things like permanent work-from-home, I have some apprehensions too. In fact, I feel it would more negatively affect women as women are increasingly seen to be choosing work-from-home while more and more men return to the office.

Natasha: Totally agree. It not only places the burden of managing home more on us, but also affects our careers as we miss out on the networking opportunities the office offers. In an ideal world, it should be the work that matters and not our presence in the office. But with the glass ceiling remaining a reality, being away from the office and not having that 'people-connect' could very much affect our career growth and promotions.

Ajay: You just echoed my fears. Many of my female friends and colleagues have time and again reiterated how 'office' is not just 'work' for them, but a very liberating experience. I think everybody, particularly women, should explore a world outside home. And office, in my opinion, is that portal which opens to a larger world.

2. Never ignore the normal world

Ajay: You seem dull. Is everything okay?

Friend: Not really.

Ajay: Would you like to share?

Friend: I had to login to a video conference last day from my home. It was an important meeting, but there I was struggling with unmuting myself and turning my video on. I felt like a laughing stock, an old man so out of place.

Ajay: I get your pain.

Friend: And I don't even want to start talking about my boss's video calls at the oddest of hours and situations. Technology might have been an enabler during Covid times, but it also took over everything and made things like this the norm.

Ajay: And you feel like you don't belong in this new world, is it?

Friend: All the time! Call me old-school, but I like to get ready in the morning, go to work, greet my colleagues good morning, and do my meetings in person. I don't feel comfortable with any of these new ways.

Ajay: I understand. In what is being called the new normal, remote working has become the norm and many a time you don't know who you are working with. People attend meetings in pyjamas and your boss thinks he can video call you anytime since now your home is also your workplace.

Friend: Exactly! If this is the new normal, where is the space for people like me?

Ajay: Well, in all fairness technology has kept work going in the past few years. There was no other go during the Covid period. But things have changed now and now there's no reason to continue the same way.

Friend: I'm glad you get it, Ajay.

Ajay: Of course I do. There's a section which finds it all overwhelming and yet have been adjusting to the new way to keep things going. Now that we have almost moved into a post-Covid world, this section should definitely be taken into consideration and we must make space for them as well. We have just survived the worst, all the more reason to be compassionate to everyone.

4. Age diversity at workplace

Ajay: Hey little champ! How's things going?

Cousin: I can't wait to finish school.

Ajay: You don't like school?

Cousin: School is awesome. But I have great plans lined up for after that.

Ajay: That's amazing! Mind letting me in on your plans?

Cousin: After working in a day job for the first 2-3 years, I will start my own company and be a successful entrepreneur.

Ajay: Wonderful!

Cousin: But I'm going to do a few things differently.

Ajay: How so?

Cousin: To start with I will hire only young employees. I believe innovative ideas come from young minds. Older people are set in their ways and afraid to take risks. Plus, youngsters bring fun and energy to the workplace.

Ajay: I'm not sure if that would be a great idea.

Cousin: See, this is the problem. The older you are, the more the negativity. Even my parents say no to everything.

Ajay: It's not negativity my dear, it's called experience. When you were a toddler, you wanted to touch fire, eat things you found on the floor, pull the cat's tail; And your parents said no. Do you call that negativity?

Cousin: But this is different.

Ajay: Is it? Do you think it would be wise to entirely ignore the perspectives and experience that a generation different from yours would bring in? These are people who have been in the industry for years and possess great insights. Who can mentor a new company better than them?

Cousin: But older people can be at times so patronising or dismissive of youngsters.

Ajay:	Unfortunately, there are such instances too. I disapprove of ageist behaviour. I think it is important to have age diversity as a criterion and instil a work culture which values your work and not your age. My point is, as a leader you can play a big role in eliminating this problem.
Cousin:	Yeah, I think you are right.
Ajay:	Every generation brings in something new and something valuable to an organisation. The right mix offers you a variety of skill sets - traditional as well as unconventional. It drives innovation, as well as hedges you against danger.
Cousin:	True. I promise my company too would be age diverse like yours.

5. Less prejudice, more inclusion

Rakhi: Did you hear? The common swimming pool was found all filthy today morning. Looks like a deliberate act by someone.

Ajay: Oh, that's unfortunate.

Rakhi: Everybody is saying the culprits must be those college kids who have newly rented a place in the apartment.

Ajay: Did someone see them doing it? Any CCTV visuals?

Rakhi: No. It's only a guess because people usually assume college students do such mischief.

Ajay: There's this Zen story I read recently. A wood cutter couldn't find his axe one day. He searched everywhere, but the axe was missing. The neighbour's son must have stolen it, he thought. So he looked over the compound wall and the boy was there.

Rakhi: Did he have the axe?

Ajay: No. But his body language looked like that of a thief. His speech sounded like that of a thief. His face appeared to be that of a thief.

Rakhi: Oh!

Ajay: The woodcutter's wife then came looking for him. "Found this from under our pile of woods," she said, handing over the axe to him. The man was speechless and looked over the wall again. The boy was still there. But neither his body language nor his face looked like that of a thief anymore. His speech didn't sound like that of a thief anymore.

Rakhi: I get your point.

Ajay: I'm glad. We as a society need to be more open and less prejudiced. For entrepreneurs especially, this is very relevant. Because great business opportunities could come from anywhere - an old rival, a banished client, a country or market that's notorious on other counts ... So, never rule out a possibility because of your prejudice, never lose an opportunity to your prejudice.

Karma

Doing Business

"No one who does good work will ever come to a bad end, either here or in the world to come"

1. How to be a blue ocean swimmer

Ajay: Hey! How's life after resigning from your job

Friend: I didn't resign

Ajay: But last time we spoke you mentioned you were planning to quit and be an entrepreneur

Friend: Yeah, I had an idea in my mind then. But later I found out that there were more than enough companies in that space already. Quitting my job to be an entrepreneur in an overcrowded space would be suicidal.

Ajay: Maybe you should take a dip in the blue ocean.

Friend: I'm sorry, what? I'm not a swimmer…

Ajay: Blue Ocean Strategy is the name of an interesting book by Chan Kim & Renee Mauborgne which details a marketing strategy that you could put to use.

Friend: Is it?

Ajay: Yes. Red Ocean represents industries that exist today and Blue Ocean is the space where industries don't exist yet. The strategy essentially talks about opening new market spaces and creating new demand.

Friend: Is it possible to open a new market in a space where the competition is already tough?

Ajay: If you make the right moves, absolutely. There have been several instances of Blue Oceans evolving from Red Oceans. Have you heard of the story of Cirque du Soleil, the largest contemporary circus producer in the world?

Friend: Circus company? I thought they were dying.

Ajay: Exactly. Everybody thought so. Yet, Cirque managed to succeed by offering a unique experience to the audience combining the best of both circus and theatre. They reduced costs and tapped into a new audience - adults and corporate clients - who were willing to pay much more than the traditional circus audience. In the founder's own words, they didn't just reinvent the circus, they repackaged it.

Friend: I think I'm getting a hang of it.

Ajay: Great! So think about your entrepreneurial idea once again. And remember the words of Chan Kim, co-author of the book - "The only way to beat the competition is to stop trying to beat the competition."

2. On risk appetite and future-proofing business

Ajay: Hello my restaurateur friend! Yesterday I got a chance to taste your food and it was absolutely delicious!

Friend: So glad to hear that!

Ajay: I'm sure it would be impossible to find someone with a different opinion. So what's your next plan?

Friend: The menu is a hit. So I was thinking I'll just stick to it.

Ajay: Well it's been a while, so why not experiment something? Add a few new items to the menu or something like that?

Friend: I'm a bit apprehensive about it. Customers love what we are offering now. So why take a risk?

Ajay: It's a safe option. For now. But what about the future?

Friend: If people love it today, won't they love it tomorrow also?

Ajay: That's one possibility. There are food joints that have gone on to become legends by offering what they have always served. But from an entrepreneur's point of view, I have also seen companies, who were once market leaders, being late to the party or left behind because they tried to play it too safe.

Friend: Really?

Ajay: Yes. Customer is the king. But when you hold on too tight to that dogma, you might not see an emerging market.

Friend: Oh!

Ajay: Xerox was the market leader in copy machines. But it wasn't the one to lead the small tabletop copier market. It was Canon.

Friend: Why?

Ajay: Because Xerox's customer-base was mostly large photocopying centres and they had no use for the small copiers. And the company let its existing customers dictate their approach entirely. There are many more such examples.

Friend: Hmm.. I guess nothing wrong in adding a few new items to the menu.

Ajay: That's entirely your discretion. All I'm saying is markets change, technologies change, customers also change. If you can foresee that and not let yourself be entirely dictated by the customers of the present, you can always stay ahead of the game. It's your choice if you want to simply stay safe or be the one to create new markets.

3. The story of two cheese sellers

As my friend and I were enjoying a fine evening at his home sipping a coffee, his 10-year-old walked in. In that adorable sing-song voice of hers, she asked ...
Uncle, would you like to hear a funny story?

Ajay: Of course dear. We all could use more laughs in our lives.
Girl: A big supermarket had been selling cheese for $ 1000 per kg. One day its owner spotted a small grocery shop in the opposite lane with a board saying '1 kg cheese at $ 750'.

Ajay: Interesting. Then?
Girl: The supermarket guy immediately reduced the price to $ 500/kg. Then the grocery shop guy reduced it to $ 250. This went on for a while. The first guy then walked up to the second guy and yelled, "Are you a fool? I can afford to give any amount of discount I like. But your business is small. If you try to imitate me, you will end up in losses." Can you guess what the grocery owner replied?

Ajay: Umm.. mind your own business?
Girl: No. He said, "I won't have any losses either, because I don't sell any Cheese!"

Ajay: Haha! That's a very interesting one!

Friend: Lol! Don't encourage her. Else you will have to listen to more silly stories like these.

Ajay: What do you mean 'silly?' It's a great story on why you should avoid indulging in unnecessary competition.

Friend: C'mon!

Ajay: Think about it. We all have this tendency to slash the prices of our products/services when we see our competitor is offering something similar at a reduced price. But what we often forget is that quality doesn't come cheap. When we short sell ourselves, we actually end up losing. And not just financial losses. The customer will fail to see the value of what you are offering and will expect to get products from you in the future too at dirt cheap prices. So if you are offering something premium, have the confidence to charge it premium. Ignore the rest. Customers who look for quality will definitely come knocking.

Friend: I see your point! (Turning to daughter) Darling, read me more often from your storybook, will you?

4. Blessed are those who have great rivals

Ajay: Hey, congrats!

Friend: Phew! What a win! This is history. Now, Lionel Messi can heave a great sigh of relief, along with millions of fans of Argentinian football!

Ajay: He certainly can. Argentina lifting the Copa America 2021 trophy this weekend, literally ends what many people called a 'trophy drought' for the ace footballer.

Friend: Yes, persistence pays. Their victory reminds me of the story of Bruce and the Spider. Argentina had to wait for decades to lift a coveted international title. Try they did! And that's great motivation for us entrepreneurs.

Ajay: Yes indeed. But I feel beyond the obvious lessons, Messi and Argentina's win offers an important insight.

Friend: I'm all ears ...

Ajay: Well, this victory was made possible by Brazil, in a way.

Friend: Eh! How?

Ajay: The takeaway here is that your excellence in performance is influenced heavily by how your rival performs. Here, Brazil's soccer team has been improving its game, posing formidable challenges to arch-rival Argentina, forcing Messi and his boys to constantly up the ante.

Friend: Interesting!

Ajay: In business, it is great to have a healthy rival who can make you sweat creatively and raise your standards so you can garner the right degree of skills, timing, strategy and resources to beat it and become the champion. Now, Brazil also benefits; it has to go back to the drawing board and re-strategize. Helps save it from saturation and complacency. On that cue, this is not a win. It's a win-win!

5. Enhance value for your clients

Ajay: What a pretty garden you have got!

Relative: All thanks to this plant seller I recently came across on the internet. Buying from him was one of the best purchasing decisions I ever made. Not only did he send me healthy plants packed carefully, once they reached here, he also gave me tips on how to care for each plant and followed up their growth every now and then. He is also available round the clock on the phone to address your queries. I was reluctant to buy plants online earlier, but since then all my orders have gone to this guy.

Ajay: Wow! Sounds like along with healthy plants, he also gave you a crash course on the importance of providing value enhancement to customers?

Rel: Huh?

Ajay: Let me explain. By sending you good saplings he met your expectations about the value of the product. The additional services enhanced that value and made you feel that your money was well-spent right?

Rel: Yes.

Ajay: Now tell me how differently you felt about your decision to buy from him compared to your earlier purchases.

Rel: Extremely good! Given the way I have gone around and told everybody about it, I think I'm even a bit proud of myself for deciding to buy from him.

Ajay: Exactly. Not only did he manage to gain a loyal customer, but you have also been campaigning for him. Your word of mouth is the most trustworthy form of marketing he can get. See the power of a great product when coupled with value enhancement?

Rel: Fascinating!

Ajay: Isn't it? Now give me some of your roses. My daughters would love them!

6. What does a haircut and Microsoft have in common

Ajay: Hey, is that a new haircut?

Colleague: Yeah. My daughter said my old looks were getting a bit too boring and got me to get a makeover.

Ajay: She isn't wrong, you know? Be it an individual or an organization, constant innovation and re-innovation are important.

Coll: What has a snip here and a snip there got to do with innovation? Don't we talk about innovation in much more serious and larger contexts?

Ajay: Innovation is a mentality, my friend. It's an attitude that reflects in your personality and in everything you do, including how you run your organization.

Coll: Care to elaborate?

Ajay: Think about it this way. You may be a handsome chap, but would you be appreciated if you walk around flaunting a hairstyle or an attire that's a decade old? Your poor choice will undermine even your greatest features. So you need to upgrade yourself according to the changing times, else you will be written off as obsolete. In other words, you need to constantly innovate yourself to become a man of the 21st century. Now replace 'you' with an organization, say Microsoft. It has the most used and most appreciated operating system across the world. But it didn't come this far with just Windows 98 or Windows XP or even Windows 10 for that matter. Of course, all these operating systems garnered a lot of goodwill, but Microsoft kept innovating, built on that goodwill, and has recently released Windows11 version, for which the world had been eagerly waiting.

Coll: That was a real eye-opener!

Ajay: And that's a really good haircut you have there!

7. Gen-z, your new brand ambassadors

Khaled: These new kids are bizarre!

Ajay: What happened?

Khaled: A few of us were having a water cooler chat. The new trainee walked by and asked us to spill the tea. Why would we!

Ajay: Haha! He wasn't asking you to spill tea literally. In Gen Z slang, it means to share the gossip.

Khaled: Why can't they just talk normally?

Ajay: For them, this is normal. Generations, as well as their language, evolve and we should be more receptive to it. In fact, instead of dismissing them, it's important for us to rejig our strategies to make our brand more visible to them.

Khaled: How?

Ajay: Many ways. To start with, they are the digital native generation with a constant presence on channels like Instagram or TikTok. So, be where they are.

Khaled: You mean, move your ads from traditional media to these channels?

Ajay: Yes and no. Traditional ad formats don't work with Gen Z. But they understand influencers. So one strategy could be promoting your brand through these influencers. Also, the old one-way communication has become obsolete. Gen Z is all about engagement, interactivity, user experience, and unique content. This means your campaign should not only be unique, but you should be able to make your product an experience for them, something about which they can tell stories and share experiences on social media. Constantly engage them, be on top of trends and talk about the causes they care about. But there's no way you can fake it with this woke generation. So be real, honest and accountable. Get them to trust you, build a community and Gen Z will become your brand ambassadors.

8. Data vs intuition

Ajay: How did the parent-teacher session go yesterday?

Shadi: My son has made me proud again. Teachers have only good things to say about him. But there was something really interesting this time.

Ajay: What was that?

Shadi: During the orientation session, a teacher came up with a fantastic presentation on the parent's role in the child's education. It was fascinating how she supported all her arguments with the help of data collected from a small sample survey.

Ajay: That's the power of data. Look around and you can see how companies that are data-driven truly stand out from the rest. For example, Amazon, where even the smallest of the decisions are taken based on data. Data gives you plain facts and nothing else. It doesn't lie.

Shadi: I have always felt that being data-driven makes you more confident and provides you with clarity.

Ajay: Indeed. Because everything other than data are just opinions. Opinions differ from person to person. But data is consistent.

Shadi: But, are you saying that one should not follow his gut?

Ajay: Not at all. The more you have been in the business the stronger will be your intuitions. Also, budding entrepreneurs who don't have enough data at their disposal might have nothing but their instincts to fall back on. But when your competitor is out there basing every decision of his on data, you can't afford to rely simply on your intuitions. Cross-verify them with what the data says. Adopt a hybrid approach if you like. But if a situation arises where you have to choose between intuition and data, I would say, always pick data. After all, they don't say data is the new oil for nothing.

Work Culture

"What is work and what is not work are questions that perplex the wisest of men"

1. The art of managing emotions

Ajay: How's everything at your startup?
Friend: Can't complain ... I guess.

Ajay: Not exactly what I expected from a young budding entrepreneur.
Friend: Well, the problem I'm facing, it's a little difficult to explain and probably more difficult to understand.

Ajay: Try me.
Friend: You know that when I started this company I didn't want it to be a stressful workplace for my staff. I wanted people to feel belonged. I wanted myself to be a really supportive and empathetic leader.

Ajay: I'm sure you are.
Friend: I understand what big a problem stress at the workplace is. So, I listen to my employees and try to address problems by taking their emotions also into account. And yet, in the recent survey conducted by our HR, a lot of employees felt that their feelings were not rightly addressed.

Ajay: First of all, kudos to your good intentions. Now coming to the problem, it is indeed a complex one. I feel the missing element here could be emotional agility.

Friend: Agility?

Ajay: Yes, it's something I read about a few years back. You mentioned earlier how stress is common in workplaces. But stress is a generalised term. To solve the problem, we need to go beyond it, take a more nuanced approach and be agile in our understanding.

Friend: I don't understand.

Ajay: Imagine an employee who is angry with a team approaches you. You try to address his anger. But is anger the only emotion he is going through? Is he sad? Anxious? What exactly caused his anger? Was he disappointed by the other team's performance? Or did they offend him? Did he get irritated with some of them slacking off?

Friend: Wow! It never occurred to me to go this deep.

Ajay: This way you are not just looking at 'anger', but more precise emotions like anxiety, disappointment, offence and so on. This kind of precision in understanding emotions will help you a great deal in interacting with your colleagues and taking the correct approach. Psychologists call it labelling our emotions. It's not easy, but it's not unachievable either. Try it out and make your office that happy place you wanted it to be.

2. Small wins are beautiful too

Ajay: Hello! Was that your son earlier inside your cabin?

Friend: Yeah, he has joined a media organisation. Today his first news story is out and he came to tell me that.

Ajay: That's wonderful! You must be very proud.

Friend: It is no big deal. He is just a cub reporter as of now. It's a long road ahead of him.

Ajay: It sure is. But that doesn't mean the small wins are meaningless.

Friend: Yeah. But shouldn't your focus be on the larger goal?

Ajay: How do you reach the larger goal without enjoying the everyday work and the small progresses you make? We humans always look for a purpose and it's very important for our productivity that we feel we are doing meaningful work.

Friend: That's true.

Ajay:	Do you know what Steve Job's pitch to John Sculley was to rope him in as Apple's new CEO?
Friend:	No...
Ajay:	Before Apple, Sculley was the President of PepsiCo. Apparently Jobs asked him if he wanted to spend the rest of his life selling sugared water or if he wanted a chance to change the world. PepsiCo is a very reputed company, no doubt about that. But what Jobs did was aim for that time immemorial quest of humans for meaning.
Friend:	I get your point.
Ajay:	You may be a father or a team leader or an entrepreneur. It's very important on your part to let your son or colleagues or employees know how much their work is contributing. It's normal for people to get demotivated and feel the work they are doing is nothing. It's your job then to show them how much value they add through the work they do every day and make them feel that the small progresses and the little wins matter.

3. The great resignation

Kader: Why is everybody suddenly resigning! People around me are quitting their jobs left, right and centre! Friends, colleagues, juniors, seniors … it's a mass exodus!

Ajay: Ah yes. You are referring to the 'Great Resignation'.

Kader: I don't understand. At the beginning of the pandemic there were mass layoffs, and whoever escaped the cull felt lucky to still have their jobs. What has changed since then?

Ajay: A pandemic is a life altering experience my friend. Do you think its impact has been limited to our health and finances? It was also a big philosophical jolt. It threw us off the track, changed the courses of our lives, forced us to recalibrate our priorities.

Kader: True. But how did that lead to mass resignations?

Ajay: Simple. Employees changed, employers didn't. The pandemic has made people realise there are bigger things than the monthly salary - work-life balance, job satisfaction, flexibility, belongingness, long term career value and growth … As employee priorities have changed, companies can't hold back their staff anymore with compensation alone. Take a closer look; you won't see much attrition at companies who treat their employees well and make them feel belonged.

Kader: Yeah, I think you are right.

Ajay: We are going through a great transition. Old ways need to change. If you don't prioritise your people, they won't prioritise you anymore. Because, as Murakami wrote, when you come out of the storm, you won't be the same person who walked in.

4. Building a great workplace - Part 1

Friend: Ajay, I need your advice.
Ajay: Sure.

Friend: The churn rate at my company has spiked recently and I can't identify where the problem lies. We offer great salaries, great perks, and provide all kinds of amenities at the office. Yet, something seems to be wrong.
Ajay: What about the workplace culture? Have you checked if there are bullies in your office?

Friend: Bullies? Like those kids who grabbed our lunch boxes and teased our appearance when we were in school?
Ajay: Yes.

Friend: I thought we were past all that when we graduated.
Ajay: Not really. Bullies are quite common in work places too. In fact reports suggest that the bullying behaviour has only gone up with remote work becoming a norm in the post-pandemic world.

Friend: Really? Why?

Ajay: Because it's easier to be aggressive when you are sitting behind a computer screen and not facing someone. Haven't you observed people who are seemingly nice otherwise turning extremely toxic on social media?

Friend: Oh, indeed.

Ajay: Online or offline, this behaviour has to be checked because surveys have found out that 'toxic corporate culture' is the single biggest predictor of employee attrition.

Friend: Not low wages?

Ajay: Nope. People have started giving more importance, and rightly so, to factors other than compensation, like mental health and work life balance. Employees no longer tolerate bullying from managers or team leads for the high pay cheques they receive. And once somebody calls it quits, then in no time it could turn into a house of cards.

Friend: I need to nip it in the bud before it gets any worse. How do I spot these bullies?

Ajay: Keep an eye out for behaviours like berating people, making them overwork, taking credit for others' work, belittling their efforts in front of others, intimidating them, isolating them, making personal remarks and defaming them through lying or any other means. Collect feedback from employees and make things more transparent. Keep your door open and allow people to directly come to you. Build confidence in them so they can talk to you. In no time will you see the bullies receding and your office once again becoming a happy place.

5. Building a great workplace - Part 2

Friend: Hey, Ajay! I owe you big time!

Ajay: You look jubilant!

Friend: That tip you gave me really worked. I started looking out for bullies at my company, took some measures to check it and the churn rates have significantly come down.

Ajay: I'm glad I could help.

Friend: You also mentioned how people have started valuing other things over wages and the importance of maintaining a good work culture. So is there some thumb rule you follow to ensure that your company is a great place for people to build their career?

Ajay: Yes, you can use the 'ABC rule'.

Friend: Sounds interesting! What does it stand for?

Ajay: Acceptance, Belongingness and Creativity.

Friend: Would you mind elaborating?

Ajay: No.1 - Accept people for who they are. An organisation will have people with different backgrounds, different perspectives, different ideas and different approaches. Do not try to turn them all into some bots cast in the same mould. Your company will benefit a great deal from diversity, your employees will learn a lot from each other and your office will be a delightful place to work.

Friend: Totally agree.

Ajay: No.2 - Make them feel belonged. You didn't singlehandedly build your company ground up. Your employees' hard work has contributed to it significantly. So, give them the due credit. Reward their work. Show them compassion. Instead of sitting in an ivory throne and passing orders, make them feel this is their company too. People give their 200 percent to something when they feel belonged.

Friend: Absolutely. And no.3?

Ajay: Allow space for people's creativity. Sure, things might have worked a certain way for long. But that doesn't mean a new way wouldn't. Your product or service might have been a great hit, but you stick to the same thing and you are practically waiting to bite the dust. So allow and encourage creativity at your workplace. Let people know their creative juices can flow. A space where people can be creative and innovative is what motivates them the most.

Friend: Brilliant! You wouldn't mind if I implemented the same at my office, would you?

Ajay: My friend, we all get to the peak together, or we don't get there at all.

In the age of internet and technology

"Calmness, gentleness, silence, self-restraint, and purity: these are the disciplines of the mind."

1. Knot your business, say no to cyber bullying

Maz and I were relishing a coffee when a colleague walked in laughing his heart out. We were curious and asked him to share the joke. What ensued was an interesting conversation.

Colleague: Ha ha! did you see this meme about Bill and Melinda Gates getting divorced? It's hilarious.

Ajay: No offence, but I think it's cruel. Someone's marriage, as well as divorce, are deeply personal matters. It shouldn't be anyone else's affair.

Colleague: But Bill and Melinda are not just anybody right? Yes, the memes may be a bit cruel, but they are just jokes. And these guys are this billionaire, celebrity, philanthropy couple. We could say they practically have shaped how the health sector across the globe functions today. Do you think this divorce is going to be without consequences? I feel these people should have thought it over.

Maz: That's quite an observation! So you are saying the people who built an entire tech empire and established a charitable trust that manages $50 billion haven't thought through their decision to go separate ways

Colleague: I don't know. Divorces are ugly. I feel that they shouldn't have done this, at least for the sake of the non-profits across the world. The Gates are the biggest charitable donors of the US and this split is going to affect the cash flow and functioning of several NGOs out there.

Ajay: Your concern might not be misplaced. But I think if you read their statements closer you might get a bit more clarity on that front. Yes, they are intending to go their separate ways personally, but they have made it clear they would continue their work together at the foundation. Also, the money managed by the foundation cannot be redirected or revoked.

Colleague: Hmm...that's comforting. But what about the approximate $150 billion that's estimated to be Gates' wealth?

Ajay: We can presume that will be split between the couple.

Colleague: My point is that what if each of them chooses to spend that money differently after the divorce? A decade ago, they had committed the majority of their assets to the foundation. We can't be sure they would stick to it after the divorce. The money that would have otherwise gone to a common cause over the years might now go to Pivotal Ventures or Gates Ventures which are Melinda and Bill's respective personal investment ventures.

Maz: Possible. But, think about what happened after the Bezos divorce in 2019. Mackenzie Scott,

Jeff Bezos's ex-wife, was giving away $1 billion a month towards charity by the end of 2020 making her one of those billionaires who was giving away her money the fastest. Just think about it, the wealth of the richest of the rich increased staggeringly during the pandemic. It was at a time like this that Scott was donating her money at such a fast pace putting pressure on her fellow billionaire philanthropists to emulate her. What more? Months after the divorce, she signed the Giving Pledge by none other than the Gates, committing at least half of her wealth to philanthropy. This was something she and Bezos had refused to do when they were a couple. Bezos still hasn't signed the pledge, while we have seen Scott becoming more and more active and vocal about philanthropy.

Ajay: So you see, good things do come out of even seemingly bad scenarios. My point is, divorce is not the end of life. And no matter how it goes, it's not something to joke about or make memes about. As members of the business fraternity and as fellow human beings, we have to not only stay away from this ridiculing behaviour but should also call out those cyber bullies. Maybe a divorce is an opportunity for someone to be happier and thus be a more productive and useful person in the world out there. Isn't that what makes all the difference at the end of the day?

2. How AI will impact the future of work, and life

Friend: Hey, Ajay! I wanted to ask you something

Ajay: Sure! Go on.

Friend: Do you think robots would take over one day?

Ajay: You mean the rise of the robots and enslavement of humans? I would say an interesting plot for a story.

Friend: So you think it's not going to happen?

Ajay: Not the way you put it. But I recently read a book called Scary Smart by Mo Gawdat and it piqued my interest. It says AI will be a billion times more intelligent than humans.

Friend: And that doesn't scare you?

Ajay: Let's try to see it this way. Who created AI?

Friend: Humans.

Ajay: Exactly. AI might not be a living being. But it is intelligent and smart. It learns and understands based on the inputs we give them. But who gives these inputs?

Friend: Again, us. Humans.

Ajay: Correct. Unfortunately the human world is imperfect and we humans are flawed. Which means our biases, prejudices and discriminatory attitudes will reflect in AI too. Reading that along with the prediction that AI is going to be billion times faster than us in a few years, doesn't paint a very rosy picture of the future.

Friend: So, in some sense we are creating a Frankenstein's monster.

Ajay: Well, I believe in a bright future. And we know AI is here to stay. So, it all depends on how we decide to treat and nurture AI. How a person turns out to be as an adult depends a lot on how s/he was raised, right? This is applicable to AI also and what we decide to feed it.

Friend: You are right.

Ajay: My point is, the future is being built by us, not by AI. It's only a tool. So, it's totally up to us as to what kind of future we want for ourselves and for the future generations. If we decide to choose compassion and respect for each other, the same would reflect in AI and that would translate into building a great world for everyone.

3. Why social media discretion is important

Ajay: Hey! You okay? Sounds like some angry typing.

Friend: Just doing some venting on social media, Ajay.

Ajay: I don't mean to intrude, but I have been seeing you posting some really angry stuff recently.

Friend: Just speaking my mind.

Ajay: But do you think it's a great idea to put it all out there?

Friend: What's wrong in expressing myself? My profile is my personal space.

Ajay: Your personal space, yes. But visible to the public. Did you hear about the Kanye West-Trevor Noah incident? Instagram suspended West's account for a day for using racial slurs against Noah.

Friend: Oh!

Ajay: Your profile is not your diary. Now that social media has given us all a platform to publish ourselves, we have, in some sense, become the social media age equivalent of traditional publishers. Now think about this, would a publisher or a newspaper editor put everything he/she feels in the publication?

Friend: No.

Ajay: The content we get comes after many levels of filtering, screening and scrutiny. They apply discretion and good sense to it. The same is applicable when we post on social media too.

Friend: I hadn't thought of it that way.

Ajay: That's just not it. Your angry tweet could spread faster than you think leading to dire consequences in your personal and professional life. People have lost jobs, and been arrested. So you can't just go about saying it's your personal space. It's not as simple as that.

Friend: I'm going to take down everything right away.

Ajay: Apply some discretion. That's all. Social media is designed to fuel anger. So always think before posting something. Abusive language is neither criticism nor expressing your opinion, it's harassment. Always ask yourself if you would say the same thing you are about to post to a person's face. Be more respectful, and more kind. Today's world needs it more than ever.

4. The power of an idea

Ajay: Hey! Saw you shooting some video at the park yesterday.
Thanvir : Yeah, for my new Reels

Ajay: Reels? I thought you were a TikTok star!
Thanvir: Not since it's banned in India.

Ajay: Oh!
Thanvir: The ban episode really scared me though. I had my whole influencer career planned around TikTok and one fine day it was banned. Instagram Reels saved the day.

Ajay: That's the power of a great idea.
Thanvir: Care to elaborate?

Ajay: Sure. First tell me, what new idea did TikTok introduce to the world?
Thanvir: Umm.. short videos?

Ajay: Yes. Until then no one had thought of it or tried it. TikTok introduced it and it became a huge hit. But one day the app was banned in India. What was a rage until then soon started vanishing from the people's collective memory. Consumers, analysts and brands have all now moved on from the platform.

Thanvir: That's right. Looks like even the parent company of TikTok, Byte dance, is not keen to make any effort to re-enter the Indian market.

Ajay: Correct. But when TikTok was banned, was that the end of short videos too?

Thanvir: Definitely not. Reels took over.

Ajay: Exactly my point. TikTok was kicked out of the market; But such was its impact that the new idea they triggered continues to live on even today, powering other brands, products and services. Why? Because the idea was bigger than the brand itself and in my view that's the best legacy to leave behind.

Thanvir: Wow! Indeed.

Ajay: Our success, in many ways, is not just ours. There were great men and women who lived and died before us, legends who left legacies of their own. We are simply continuing from where they left off and building on the foundation of great ideas they contributed to the world. Now our strife should be towards giving the next big idea to the world, an idea that's bigger than ourselves, don't you think?

Thanvir: Can't agree more. And my next Reels is going to feature you.

5. Building you on social media

Friend: Social media is a scam!
Ajay: Where's that coming from?

Friend: I have been trying to build my personal brand. But my posts don't get reach or recognition and I barely have any followers. How did you do it, Ajay?
Ajay: Definitely not overnight. Tell me what your process has been.

Friend: I have profiles on all major social media platforms and whenever I have free time I post some content.
Ajay: If you want my honest opinion, that's not a very systematic approach. What you do in your free time is a hobby. Building your personal brand is not a hobby. It's serious business.

Friend: So, how should I go about it?
Ajay: First you need to be clear why you are doing this. What's your motivation? Is it because everybody around you is doing it or do you have a better purpose? If you don't have a purpose, your motivation is bound to fizzle out half way.

Friend: I should look into that.

Ajay: Once you know your purpose you will have a clear idea about how much to invest in it.

Friend: In terms of money?

Ajay: Mostly in terms of your time. When you have that kind of clarity you will also have some idea about how long it might actually take to build your brand. Remember, we are talking about years here.

Friend: Funny to think that I got frustrated in a few weeks!

Ajay: Knowing your end goals is also important. You need to ensure your posts are in alignment with what you desire to build. Adopt a more targeted approach and know what kind of audience you are looking at.

Friend: Okay.

Ajay: Above all, decide how badly you want to do this. Because here, consistency is the key. And if you are already doing a lot of things, you might have to sacrifice a thing or two for this. You need to ask yourself if you are ready for that.

Friend: Got it!

Ajay: I would say have a project manager attitude towards building your personal brand. Don't expect windfall gains. Know your goals and see how well your progress, however small it may be, compares against it. And then give yourself a pat for those small victories.

6. Is your brand well protected?

Nasir : Ajay, is that a fruit drink in your hand?

Ajay: Yup.

Nasir: I'm not sure if you should drink it. I recently read a WhatsApp message which said an employee of this juice company is polluting the drinks. I'm wondering why more people are not calling out this brand after a serious accusation like this.

Ajay: Because it's only an accusation. In other words, fake news, misinformation, or disinformation. Many businesses like this juice brand are today facing serious threats from organised disinformation campaigns. From semiconductor giants to telecom companies to restaurants... Tomorrow it could be you. So please exercise some caution before brandishing WhatsApp forwards as 'information'.

Nasir: Oh, I'm so sorry. That's very serious. Is there something businesses could do to guard against such attacks?

Ajay: Giving media literacy to each and every employee and starting awareness campaigns among customers is a good place to start. Take stock of the vulnerabilities that are specific to your organisation and then strengthen those points. Assign dedicated staff to watch the patterns in disinformation campaigns, spot the methods, monitor social media and do sentiment analysis. This would help to identify a negative campaign in its nascent stage and nick it in the bud. Have authentic and genuine conversations with your existing and potential customers. Build a positive narrative about your brand and make your customers your strongest advocates. Connect with your business partners too in a similar way. Last but not the least, have a plan ready to counter fake news campaigns. Try to anticipate in advance campaigns likely to be launched against you and practice your defence, just like how you conduct mock drills against fire hazard. Because this hazard is no less and can gut your business if you have not been careful.

Bhakti

Giving back

"Paraspara Bhava is the one that guarantees ultimate prosperity."

1. Faith in the power of entrepreneurship

Maz: So I met an aspiring entrepreneur the other day and he asked for some advice.

Ajay: Indeed, quite an exciting time to be a startup mentor!

Maz: True. You know I have seen this common notion among people that one needs to have the legacy of a family business or hail from a rich family to make it big as an entrepreneur.

Ajay: Ah, that reminds me of an interesting conversation I had with someone recently. I was asked why there is not a Google or Facebook from India?

Maz: What did you say?

Ajay: I said Why do you need a Google or Facebook from India when you have Fresh works from India?

Maz: The SaaS company?

Ajay: Yes. Headquartered in California, but founded in Chennai by Girish Mathrubootham and Shan Krishnasamy. It got listed on Nasdaq recently at a spectacular valuation of $13 billion. And all this happened in a matter of just 10 years!

Maz: That is impressive indeed. And did Mr. Mathrubhootham come from a family of entrepreneurs to pull it off within such a small period?

Ajay: He is the son of a retired bank officer. See, as you said this is where people often go wrong about entrepreneurship. To make it big as an entrepreneur, what you need is the right spirit, skills, attitude, passion, faith and ultimately a bend of mind to give it back.

Maz: Absolutely. Giving it back is so important. Most think one is in business to make profits alone.

Ajay: Profits are an important part of business, no doubt. But take this case itself. Mathrubhootham and Krishnasamy are not the only ones who made a fortune. When Freshworks got listed, around 500 of its employees too turned millionaires. In an interview some time back he revealed as saying to his wife that he started the company not because he could buy a BMW, but because his employees also could buy one. And he walked the talk. That's the right spirit of an entrepreneur. If you have that kind of spirit, no matter how humble your beginnings are, you are destined for greatness.

Maz: You are right. I guess this is yet another example that reaffirms faith in the power of entrepreneurship.

Ajay: It is indeed.

2. Think big, dream bigger

Chris Khouri : Tell me this Ajay, which entrepreneur do you find the most inspiring?

Ajay: It's impossible to say just one name. There are many, from Bill Gates to Jeff Bezos to Elon Musk to...

Chris Khouri : Haha! Interesting that all your inspirational figures are right now busy giving each other a tough time.

Ajay: What do you mean?

Chris Khouri : Well, Bezos and Musk are embroiled in a space race. Bill Gates, on the other hand, recently took a jibe at both of them in one swipe, quipping that we have a lot to do here on earth, when asked about space interests of billionaires.

Ajay: Haha, good one! After all, what's life without some wit! But on a serious note, I think both Gates and the Bezos-Musk duo are right.

Chris Khouri: How so?

Ajay: As entrepreneurs, we have a lot to do here as Gates said. We have a responsibility towards the larger society and our efforts should be towards making this world a better place for everyone. Gates is being a great role model through his efforts to improve healthcare globally. On the other hand, space exploration and related technologies have taken mankind forward by leaps and bounds. It's absolutely important that entrepreneurs play an active role in taking it further forward for the benefit of the entire humanity. So I would say, let's keep our feet firm on the earth and reach out to the stars!

3. Why intent matters

Friend: This business person I know does quite a few philanthropic activities, but also makes sure he turns it into a big spectacle. I don't know what to make out of it. What do you think, Ajay?

Ajay: Doing philanthropic activities is a great thing and, in my personal opinion, is also a responsibility of every entrepreneur.

Friend: I totally agree. But whether to flaunt it or not is my question.

Ajay: It's not that black and white. More than the action itself, it's the intent that would be important here.

Friend: I'm listening.

Ajay: Let not thy left hand know what thy right doeth, says the Bible. Karmanye vadhikaraste ma phaleshu kadachana, reads the Bhagavad Gita. The Quran too says if you do deeds of charity openly, it is well; but if you bestow it upon the needy secretly, it is even better.

Friend: Then it's pretty clear that one shouldn't advertise his own charity works, right?

Ajay: We should also take into account the fact that these scriptures were written in a time period vastly different from ours. I completely respect those who do it that way, it's very noble of them. But I also wouldn't go about judging those who openly talk about their philanthropic works.

Friend: Why so?

Ajay: Because it serves a different purpose. Entrepreneurs are influential personalities and role models to many. So when they talk about their activities, it could inspire thousands to do similar activities.

Friend: I guess I never thought of it that way.

Ajay: That's why I said the intent matters. More than what you do or how you do it, why you do it matters and it changes the meaning of your action entirely. Are you doing charity to give back to the society or to build your image? Is it a way to build your brand and reap benefits out of it or are your actions genuine? Are you piggybacking on the needy to catapult your business or are you finding a purpose in what you do? I think these are the relevant questions and you might have your answer by now.

Friend: I do. Thanks, Ajay.

Better earth

"All actions take place in time by the interweaving of the forces of Nature; but the man lost in selfish delusion thinks that he himself is the actor."

1. Time is ticking

Krishnan: Hey Ajay, I have been seeing this 'Decommission Mullaperiyar Dam' trending for the last few days on social media. I looked it up today and then only realised it was a controversy around a dam in your native place.

Ajay: Yes, Mullaperiyar dam is the first ever dam in Kerala.

Krishnan: Wow! The oldest is it? So I assume the controversy is also as big as the dam itself.

Ajay: It is indeed. But I believe the real conversation should be about stopping our over reliance on hydel power and hence on dams.

Krishnan: I'm sure you are right. But what's the alternative?

Ajay: The most obvious answer is of course renewable energy. As the world desperately tries to not miss the last chance to save humankind from going extinct, I think sustainability should be our motto in everything we do. Across the globe, governments and the private sector are seen promoting the transformation from coal and hydel power to renewable energy. I think it's high time to get rid of the obsession with traditional methods of power generation.

Krishnan: So, how do you suggest that can be done?

Ajay: I'm no expert, but why can't renewable sources be used to support all our micro, consumer power requirements? Why not tweak institutions like regional electricity boards to accommodate renewables? Some efforts are happening in that direction, but if we really put our hearts and souls into it, I feel, there's a lot more we can do to hand over the world without more damage to the future generations.

2. Should businesses care about climate change?

Ajay: COP is here!

Sameer: Why should we worry? We have never tried to cook the books.

Ajay: What?? No not cop, COP27! The 27th United Nations Climate Change conference. It's set to begin on 6th November.

Sameer: Oh! I don't pay much attention to these. I think all these talks and instructions around climate action is difficult to adhere to while doing business. We need to make profits at the end of the day, no?

Ajay: No offence my friend, but that's a very problematic and short-sighted way of viewing things.

Sameer: Why?

Ajay: Let me explain. You must have heard of the erratic rains and floods happening in Kerala?

Sameer: Of course, it has been sort of an annual phenomenon for the past 3-4 years.

Ajay: Exactly. Myopic businesses had been trying to make a quick buck by clearing forests and doing unsustainable construction activities even on ecologically fragile lands. As a result natural calamities have become common. Eventually that would result in the real estate market nose diving hitting at the core of the very same businesses.

Sameer: I get your point.

Ajay: Good, because while profits are important, so is the ground beneath your feet. Climate action is as important to a business person as it is to anyone else. Businesses should be in alignment with the climate goals and the community should pay good heed to what transpires out of COP27. Afterall, what's the point if you miss the forest for the trees?

3. E-Vehicles, the inevitable future

Murtuza: Ajay, I need your opinion on something.

Ajay: Sure. What's it about?

Murtuza: I bought a new car. It's electric.

Ajay: That's brilliant! Congrats!

Murtuza: Thanks! I too was pretty elated to buy it. But yesterday, a friend ridiculed me for buying it. Since then I have been wondering if I made a mistake.

Ajay: Why did he ridicule you?

Murtuza: Apparently e-vehicles haven't taken off as expected. They are costlier, have low mileage and lack adequate charging infrastructure, he says.

Ajay: It's true that we are yet to see many e-vehicles on the road. But that's what makes your decision futuristic. Whoever ridicules you for buying an e-car is only making a fool of himself. Yes, they are costlier. But think about the savings on other fronts you would make, like fuel expenses for instance. With climate action being a top priority of governments now, we would soon see more and more charging infrastructure also. So I assure you, there's nothing to worry about.

Murtuza: Are you sure?

Ajay: Absolutely! Electric vehicles are a growing market. Major brands like Tesla, BMW, Nissan, Chevrolet, Ford, Volkswagen, Kia are all now offering e-variants which indicates an upbeat market in the future.

Murtuza: That's true.

Ajay: Above all, think about the carbon footprint you have helped to remove from the environment by deciding to buy an e-car. You have done a service to your children and to the future generations.

Murtuza: I'm so relieved to hear that Ajay.

Ajay: No worries my friend. E-vehicles are the inevitable future. You should feel proud to be one of the early adopters paving the way for an EV revolution.

Potpourri

"I am the pure fragrance that comes from the earth and the brightness of fire I am. I am the life of all living beings, and the austere life of those who train their souls."

1. Silence isn't always golden

Ajay: "I closed my mouth and spoke to you in a hundred silent ways!" If I get a chance to reincarnate, I want to be reborn as a human, only to soak myself once again in the beauty & profoundness of mystical lines penned by great poets like Rumi.

Maz: They say his poems transcend geographies. I would say they transcend even contexts. Not just people from different places, but even people from different fields can relate to Rumi. For example, the lines you recited now make so much sense even when placed in the context of a workplace, its leadership, and staff.

Ajay: Wow, indeed! 'They close their mouth and speak to us silently.' If people at the workplace hesitate to talk or open up to us, they are indeed communicating something to us!

Maz: Exactly. Their silence tells us a hundred things like the absence of trust, encouragement, motivation, openness, and space to grow. People's silence is a loud statement on our failure as leaders.

Ajay: Yes. It's not the voices that a leader should be scared of, it's the silence. It shows simmering dissatisfaction and insecurity leading to a dysfunctional workplace. Maybe I should take a break from management books and read more of Rumi for a change!

2. Values we derive from relationships

Ajay: How was your college reunion?

Mazen: It was great! Meeting many of them after so many years! Was a wonderful feeling.

Ajay: Always good to catch up with old friends. So how are they all?

Mazen: All are doing great in life except this one person whom we all thought would make it really big in life. He used to be so good at everything, started working at a top MNC after college and then started his own company.

Ajay: That sounds great!

Mazen: But, eventually he just cut contacts with us friends. I heard he withdrew from other social circles too except those which were directly related to his work. Somewhere in between all this, his relation with his family also went sour.

Ajay: Now that sounds like many I know…

Mazen: People around him say he did all that to fully focus on work, but unfortunately his company also is not doing very well now. That's really surprising.

Ajay: I think the problem lies in seeing things in isolation and making monetary goals one's sole focus. Human relationships are beautiful. Family, friends, classmates, neighbours, acquaintances, other special people in our lives ... there are so many values we derive from such relationships.

Mazen: Yes, but what exactly do we learn?

Ajay: Where do we learn our interpersonal skills? Where do we learn how to handle people? Where do we learn trust, compassion, management, judgement skills? From our relationships, heritage and culture, right? An entrepreneur's life is about value generation. Therefore s/he, instead of shunning these things, should embrace them. Derive value from wherever possible. Because that makes us better entrepreneurs, better humans.

3. What to do when life throws a curveball

Ajay: Hi! I heard the news and thought I'll check on you. How are you?

Friend: Hit by quite a curveball. I fear losses of this kind could be the end of the business I have built painstakingly over the years.

Ajay: C'mon! You are a spirited entrepreneur.

Friend: I don't know Ajay. This pain makes me so weak. I hate the idea of being so vulnerable.

Ajay: Pain doesn't make you vulnerable, it makes you human. It means you haven't gone numb, that you still care for things, that your life is meaningful. If you don't feel pain, it means you have been simply existing and not really living life in its full sense.

Friend: Maybe. But to go through this phase is tough.

Ajay: I know. Trust me, we all have been there. But imagine if it was a physical pain, say a headache. What would you have done?

Friend: Take medication to cure it, avoid triggers in the future ...

Ajay: Exactly. When you feel pain, you see there's a problem and give attention to it. You find ways to overcome it and take steps to avoid it in the future. The same applies here too. Pain is not an indication that it's time to give up. Pain means you value things, you sense the loss. With the right approach and attitude, pain lets you grow stronger.

Friend: I guess you are right. Thanks Ajay, I feel so much better.

Ajay: Life might not always be hunky-dory my friend. Afterall remember what Nietzsche said, to live is to suffer, to survive is to find meaning in suffering. Let's keep pursuing that meaning and take the rest in stride.

4. Creativity spurred by boredom

Ajay: Hey! You are back! How did the vacation go?

Mark: Not great. There were too many Covid cases and I didn't feel it was safe to travel anywhere. So I was just stuck at home, all bored.

Ajay: You know, boredom always might not be that bad.

Mark: How is that? When we don't do anything, aren't we wasting our time?

Ajay: It's true that we entrepreneurs try to be as productive as possible and make the most out of every second. But I recently came across this book which says how with an adaptive approach boredom could in fact motivate us.

Mark: Which book is this?

Ajay: Out of My Skull by James Danckert and John D Eastwood. According to the book it is beneficial to have the capacity to be bored because unlike the common perception boredom could actually spur creativity.

Mark: But how?

Ajay: According to the authors, boredom is the state in which you want to do something interesting, but somehow you just can't. It's when you are bored of something that you want to actually do more or do something different right? And it's that desire that has built civilisations and led innovations. So, instead of feeling bad about being bored, what if we entrepreneurs, who are surrounded by a lot of ideas, consider it a cleansing exercise?

Mark: Amazing thought. Definitely going to try that out!

5. New year, new goals

Ajay: Hello dear! So, what are your new year resolutions? Care to share?

Jahnavi: Resolutions? C'mon dad, who cares about those things anymore? They have become so obsolete.

Ajay: Since when?

Jahnavi: Since always. It's a useless exercise.

Ajay: Well, at the risk of sounding 'obsolete', I would say I still consider new year resolutions important.

Jahnavi: But why??

Ajay: Taking resolutions is all about setting targets. You are an ambitious young girl who wishes to live a meaningful life. For you, the New Year's resolution is not a cliched ritual, but an opportunity to review the year that has passed, analyse where you stand now, set new goals based on that and pursue them with renewed vigour.

Jahnavi: But dad, who adheres to these resolutions?

Ajay: We all try. And if we fail, that's still okay. We then know where we failed, what our weakness is and what we should work on.

Jahnavi: I never thought of it that way.

Ajay: Just look at the sheer variety of human ambitions, my dear; Eat healthy, start a new hobby, travel more, make new friends, learn to say no, find a better job, take up a new course, write a book, spend more time with kids, adopt a puppy, make that entrepreneurial plunge, build a new product... If you ask me, these dreams and goals, the constant quest for a purpose in life and the sheer will to pursue them relentlessly make our existence beautiful. And a resolution is all about that.

Jahnavi: These words are the best New Year gift I could get. Thanks dad!

Ajay: Happy new year my girl! Wishing you joy, happiness and all the best things in life!

6. The larger picture

Huzefa: Hey Ajay, I have been meaning to ask you something.

Ajay: Shoot!

Huzefa: I have seen this globe in your cabin, and last day I saw you looking at it. It got me so curious. What on earth could you be looking at on a globe when you have all the information about every nook and corner of the earth on your phone?

Ajay: Hahaha! I'm glad you asked this. Let me show you. On this globe, try to locate the exact spot we are in now.

Huzefa: How's that possible? It would be a very tiny spot on this globe, probably invisible to our eyes.

Ajay: Exactly. This globe tells us that we are tiny beings who are individually insignificant in the larger scheme of things. But at the same time, collectively, the human race has revolutionised the world, isn't it? Tells you a lot about the power of the team. So, looking at the globe is simultaneously a humbling experience as well as a proud moment.

Huzefa: That's amazing! It really puts things in perspective.

Ajay: It's a very spiritual experience. You try it out too. In fact, every aspiring entrepreneur should. Because only the globe lets you view the earth in its entirety, reminding you to think about the larger picture. It tells you about the distances we can cover if we work together as a team. It shows you there's a much larger world out there, so much more for us to see, so much more for us to learn and so much more for us to do. As Robert Frost wrote, miles and miles to go, my friend, miles and miles.

7. Philosophy and entrepreneurship

A friend walked in as I was enjoying a book recently. An interesting conversation followed that went on like this...

Bilal: So it's true that you are a voracious reader.

Ajay: I just like to think of myself as a 'forever student'. And who can be better teachers than books!

Bilal: Great! So, what are you reading now?

Ajay: The story of philosophy by Will Durant.

Bilal: Now I'm intrigued. How does reading philosophy help an entrepreneur?

Ajay: Doesn't it? Think about it. To start with, isn't the vision and mission of your organisation largely influenced by your philosophy of life? Or are they just plaques displayed in your reception area?

Bilal: No, not at all. Tell me more.

Ajay:	Be it in our personal or professional lives, every step of ours is guided by our philosophy and outlook of life. Are you able to stay calm when things around you seem to go haywire? When you make strategic decisions how objectively are you able to think? Are you able to work on even the smallest detail keeping the larger picture in mind? How do you handle arguments or debates in your office?
Bilal:	Yeah, these are all difficult situations.
Ajay:	Yes. And it's your philosophical clarity that will come to your aid in such difficult situations. Because philosophy lets you step out of yourself and see things objectively. It helps us to constantly review and renew our ways, decisions and thought processes. Because as Socrates said, the unexamined life is not worth living!

A NOTE OF GRATITUDE!

Let me tell you a Zen story.

One night, a thief entered a Zen guru's shrine. The master was meditating. Wielding a knife, the intruder asked for money. The Zen guru said: "Take money from the drawer. But don't disturb my meditation." The man was astonished to see the fearlessness of the master. He took all the money. But the guru said: "Leave some; I need to buy my food tomorrow." The thief was surprised again. He left some in the box and prepared to leave. "What do you tell someone when you get a gift?" asked the guru then. "Thank you!" said the thief before leaving.

A few days later, the thief was caught by the police and they recovered the Zen master's money from him. Planning to punish the robber, the cops called the master as a witness. But the guru smiled. "This man is no thief to me; I had given him money and he thanked me for it." The cops had to let him off, but soon the thief joined the Master and became a monk.

Gratitude, as the Zen story tells us, is a bigger force than anything else in your life. It's something that adds value to your 'takings'. It tells you that whatever you have is not exactly or entirely yours. You take from others. The world feeds you with ideas, emotions, wealth and, above all, wisdom.

Be grateful.

Every milestone I cross, I am indebted to a bouquet of people. And first on the list are my parents. They both were teachers and they taught me a lot about life, especially the most fundamental rule of being a human being, which is to be 'humane'. They taught me the art of communication as well. They taught me to have clarity of thought in everything I do. I owe them a lot. This book is a result of the lessons they imparted on parenting, teaching, sharing and caring. Thank you achan & amma.

Next, a big thank you to my better, bolder and wiser half, Rakhi. She holds a mirror up to me and makes me see myself in the right shape and form, raw and real and keeps me grounded and rooted. She completes me. She is the book I read every day, from which I learn, re-learn and unlearn. Along with my children, Aparna and Jahnavi, who blend meaning into my mundane existence, Rakhi has blessed me with a family that I want to call a university of pragmatic wisdom. Every word I write or speak has a stamp of this institution. Thank you dear ones, this book would not have happened without your support.

I'm nobody without the support of my well-wishers and friends, especially the 'DHRUKAM' force of Dinesh, Hari, Rajeev, Unni, Krishnan and Manoj. You folks bring out the best in me and you are the corrective force and propelling power behind my audacious, ambitious ventures. I dedicate this to our friendship and camaraderie. Manoj (Mannan), I know you're smiling at me reading this in your heavenly abode. Need all your blessings, buddy.

I must extend a warm hug and shake hands with my colleagues at Emircom for their support, especially the wonderful Mohamad Abou Zaki, who is more than a colleague, but a friend in need and deed, a philosopher and a great fellow soldier. Thank you dear Maz!

Finally, thank you Huzefa Fakhruddin, for your unconditional support, for your organizing abilities, patience and sense of duty.

Yours,

Ajayya Kumar